OF THE
BIBLE

Text copyright © 1998 by Carolyn Larsen
Illustrations copyright © 1998 by Dennis Edwards
Edited by Shari TeSlaa

Produced by Educational Publishing Concepts, Inc. Wheaton, Illinois.
Published by New Kids Media™ in association with Baker Book House
Company, P.O. Box 6287 Grand Rapids, Michigan 49516-6287.

Printed in the United States of America. All rights reserved.

1 2 3 4 5 6 7 — 01 00 99 98

OF THE
BIBLE

Written by
Carolyn Larsen
Illustrated by
Dennis Edwards

published in
association with

BAKER
A DIVISION OF
Baker Book House Co

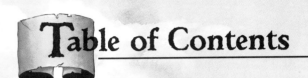

Table of Contents

Old Testament

New Testament

The Old Testament

Something From Nothing

GENESIS 1:1–2:3

LIGHT EXPLODED INTO THE DARKNESS. GOD SAW THE LIGHT WAS GOOD. HE CALLED THE LIGHT DAY AND THE DARKNESS NIGHT. THE FIRST DAY OF CREATION ENDED.

WATER SPLASHED AND GLISTENED IN THE LIGHT. WATER, WATER EVERYWHERE. GOD DIVIDED THE WATER INTO TWO SECTIONS. THE UPPER PART HE CALLED SKY. THE SECOND DAY OF CREATION ENDED.

IN THE BEGINNING THERE WAS NOTHING BUT BLACKNESS ... EMPTINESS ... SILENCE. GOD'S SPIRIT MOVED BACK AND FORTH ABOVE WATER THAT HAD NO SHAPE OR FORM. THEN GOD'S VOICE BROKE THROUGH THE DARKNESS: LET THERE BE LIGHT!

STILL THERE WAS NOTHING ON EARTH EXCEPT WATER. THE THIRD DAY, THE LOWER WATERS ROLLED AND TUMBLED AS GOD MOVED THEM TOGETHER TO MAKE OCEANS AND SEAS. DRY LAND TREMBLED AND SHOOK AS IT ROSE OUT OF THE WATERS ... GOD FILLED IT WITH ALL KINDS OF PLANTS AND TREES.

ON THE FOURTH DAY GOD SAID...
LET BRIGHT LIGHTS APPEAR IN THE SKY TO
SEPARATE THE DAY FROM THE NIGHT. THE SUN
WILL LIGHT THE DAYTIME. THE MOON AND STARS
WILL SHINE IN THE NIGHT SKY.

THE SKY AND
SEA WERE
BEAUTIFUL...
AND EMPTY. SO
GOD FILLED THE
SKY AND SEAS
WITH EVERY
IMAGINABLE
KIND OF FLYING
AND SWIMMING
CREATURE. HE
DID THIS ON THE
FIFTH DAY.

LIVESTOCK, SMALL ANIMALS AND WILDLIFE.

STILL THERE WERE NO ANIMALS OR PEOPLE ON THE LAND. BUT ON THE SIXTH DAY GOD SAID, LET THE EARTH BRING FORTH EVERY KIND OF ANIMAL.

GOD'S GREATEST CREATION CAME NEXT, ON THAT SIXTH DAY—MAN.
GOD WAS NOW FINISHED CREATING. HE WAS PLEASED WITH EVERYTHING HE HAD MADE.
ON THE SEVENTH DAY HE RESTED.

Major Trouble

GENESIS 3

ADAM AND EVE TAUGHT THEIR SONS TO SERVE GOD.

GIVE GOD THE FIRST AND BEST OF WHATEVER YOU HAVE. SHOW HIM THAT YOU ARE TRULY THANKFUL FOR ALL HE GIVES YOU.

WHEN CAIN AND ABEL GREW UP ABEL BECAME A SHEPHERD AND CAIN BECAME A FARMER.

LORD GOD, I GIVE YOU THE BEST PARTS OF THIS FIRSTBORN LAMB AS AN OFFERING OF THANKS FOR ALL YOU HAVE DONE FOR ME.

AHHH. IF ABEL IS GIVING A SACRIFICE, I GUESS I MUST GIVE ONE ALSO.

Rotten to the Core

GENESIS 6:1–7:5

ADAM AND EVE HAD MORE CHILDREN AND SOON THE EARTH WAS FILLED WITH PEOPLE . . . BAD PEOPLE.

PEOPLE WHO WORSHIPED IDOLS INSTEAD OF GOD. PEOPLE WHO LIED, STOLE, MURDERED.

NOAH WAS THE ONLY MAN WHO STILL SERVED GOD.

Top Two Worst Places to Live

GENESIS 19:1-29

PEOPLE OBEYED GOD FOR A WHILE AFTER THE FLOOD. BUT GENERATIONS PASSED AND PEOPLE OBEYED GOD LESS AND LESS. FOR EXAMPLE . . .

WELCOME TO SODOM, STRANGERS. MY NAME IS LOT. YOU'RE WELCOME TO STAY AT MY HOME WHILE YOU'RE IN TOWN.

HEY! DID YOU SEE THOSE TWO STRANGERS? THEY'RE STAYING AT LOT'S HOUSE.

LET'S GO GET THEM. WE CAN HAVE SOME FUN WITH THEM.

HEH HEH HEH!!!

SOON A GANG OF WICKED MEN STOOD OUTSIDE LOT'S DOOR.

THE CROWD GRABBED FOR LOT. THEY WERE ABOUT TO DRAG HIM INTO THE STREET WHEN THE TWO STRANGERS PULLED HIM BACK INTO THE HOUSE.

NO, GO AWAY. THEY ARE UNDER MY PROTECTION WHILE THEY STAY WITH ME!

GIVE US THE MEN, OR WE'LL COME IN AND GET YOU!

HEY, LOT! SEND THOSE STRANGERS OUT. WE HAVE PLANS FOR THEM!

BREAK THE DOOR DOWN! GET LOT AND THOSE STRANGERS!

AS THE MEN BEGAN TO RIOT, SOMETHING UNEXPECTED HAPPENED . . .
WHAT'S GOING ON?
MY EYES—I CAN'T SEE! HELP! HELP!
THE TWO STRANGERS WERE ACTUALLY ANGELS. THEY STRUCK THE RIOTING MEN BLIND WHILE THEY GAVE LOT A MESSAGE.
TAKE YOUR FAMILY AND LEAVE TOWN. GOD IS GOING TO DESTROY SODOM AND GOMORRAH. THERE IS TOO MUCH EVIL AND WICKEDNESS IN THESE TWO CITIES.

LOT'S WIFE COULDN'T RESIST ONE LAST LOOK AT HER FORMER HOME. WHEN SHE GLANCED BACK, SHE TURNED INTO A COLUMN OF SALT. LOT AND HIS TWO DAUGHTERS RAN AS FAST AS THEY COULD.

BY MORNING SODOM AND GOMORRAH WAS A PILE OF ASHES.

YES, FATHER?

YOU ARE THE SACRIFICE GOD HAS TOLD ME TO OFFER.

BUT FATHER . . .

SHHH. TRUST GOD, MY SON.

ABRAHAM TIED UP ISAAC AND LAID HIM ON THE ALTAR. HE SLOWLY RAISED HIS KNIFE TO SACRIFICE HIS SON. BUT . . .

ABRAHAM!

ABRAHAM!

DON'T HARM THE BOY. NOW I KNOW THAT YOU FEAR GOD. YOU DIDN'T REFUSE TO GIVE ME YOUR SON, YOUR ONLY SON.

ABRAHAM LOOKED AROUND AND SAW A RAM CAUGHT IN A BUSH. HE UNTIED ISAAC AND TOGETHER THEY SACRIFICED THE RAM TO GOD, PRAISING AND WORSHIPING HIM.

THE BROTHERS TOLD JACOB THAT A WILD ANIMAL HAD EATEN HIS FAVORITE SON, JOSEPH. THEY KILLED A GOAT, THEN TORE JOSEPH'S COAT AND DIPPED IT IN THE GOAT BLOOD BEFORE SHOWING IT TO JACOB.

YES, THIS IS JOSEPH'S COAT, STAINED WITH HIS OWN BLOOD. I WILL CRY FOR MY SON UNTIL I DIE.

It's Always Darkest Before the Dawn

GENESIS 39:1–41:37

IN EGYPT JOSEPH WAS SOLD TO POTIPHAR, CAPTAIN OF THE KING'S GUARD. IT DIDN'T TAKE LONG FOR JOSEPH TO IMPRESS POTIPHAR.

JOSEPH, I'VE SEEN HOW HARD YOU WORK. I'M PUTTING YOU IN CHARGE OF EVERYTHING I OWN.

WITH JOSEPH IN CHARGE, THINGS WENT VERY WELL IN POTIPHAR'S HOUSE. UNTIL ONE DAY WHEN POTIPHAR WAS AWAY . . .

THAT JOSEPH IS ONE GOOD-LOOKING YOUNG MAN. I WANT TO KNOW HIM BETTER . . . MUCH BETTER.

REUBEN, DID YOU NOTICE WE ARE SEATED ACCORDING TO AGE?

THIS MAN SEEMS TO KNOW A LOT ABOUT US.

THE BROTHERS ATE, BOUGHT MORE GRAIN, THEN LEFT EGYPT AGAIN. THEY HAD ONLY GONE A SHORT DISTANCE WHEN AN EGYPTIAN SOLDIER CAME RIDING AFTER THEM.

STOP!

ONE OF YOU HAS STOLEN MY MASTER'S SILVER CUP. THAT MAN MUST RETURN WITH ME TO BE A SLAVE.

A SEARCH REVEALED THE CUP IN BENJAMIN'S BAG.

OH, NO. WHAT WILL FATHER SAY? WE CAN'T GO HOME WITHOUT BENJAMIN!

GOD SENT MOSES AND AARON TO MEET PHARAOH ON THE BANKS OF THE NILE.

GOD SAYS TO LET HIS PEOPLE GO.

NO!

AARON STRUCK THE RIVER WITH HIS SHEPHERDS STAFF.

THE WATER HAS TURNED INTO BLOOD!

OOOO, IT STINKS!

ALL THE WATER IN EGYPT TURNED INTO BLOOD. IT WAS SEVEN FULL DAYS BEFORE THE WATER WAS NORMAL AGAIN.

AT MIDNIGHT THE LORD BEGAN MOVING THROUGH EGYPT.

PHARAOH, THE FIRSTBORN SONS IN ALL EGYPT ARE DEAD. EVEN YOUR OWN SON.

MY SON, OH MY SON. BRING MOSES TO ME—NOW.

TAKE YOUR PEOPLE AND ALL THEY OWN AND GET OUT OF EGYPT.

1. I am the Lord your God; never have any other God.

2. Never make your own carved idols or statues.

3. Never use the name of the LORD your God carelessly.

4. Remember the day of worship by observing it as a holy day.

5. Honor your father and your mother.

6. Never murder.

7. Never commit adultery.

8. Never steal.

9. Never lie about your neighbor.

10. Never desire to take anything that belongs to your neighbor.

WHEN MOSES CAME DOWN THE MOUNTAIN, THE PEOPLE JOINED HIM IN WORSHIPING GOD. EVERYONE AGREED TO DO ALL THAT THE LORD SAID.

Broken Promises

EXODUS 24:12-18; 32:1-24

LATER MOSES WENT BACK UP THE MOUNTAIN FOR A SECOND CONVERSATION WITH GOD. JOSHUA WENT ALONG WITH HIM.

WHAT IS WRONG WITH YOU PEOPLE? HAVE YOU FORGOTTEN EVERYTHING GOD HAS DONE FOR YOU?

JUST A FEW DAYS AGO, YOU PROMISED TO WORSHIP ONLY HIM. NOW YOU'VE BROKEN THAT PROMISE AND CHEATED HIM OF YOUR WORSHIP.

AARON, HOW DID YOU LET THEM TALK YOU INTO THIS?

THE PEOPLE THOUGHT YOU WERE NEVER COMING BACK. THEY GAVE ME JEWELRY, AND I THREW IT INTO THE FIRE—AND THIS CALF IS WHAT CAME OUT.

MELT DOWN THAT STATUE!

MOSES GROUND THE GOLD INTO DUST AND SPRINKLED IT ON THE WATER.

DRINK THIS WATER—EVERY ONE OF YOU.

BUT IT WILL MAKE US SICK.

DRINK IT! AND THINK ABOUT HOW YOU'VE DISOBEYED GOD.

I HAVE TO GO BACK UP THE MOUNTAIN AND ASK GOD TO FORGIVE YOU.

GOD DID FORGIVE THE ISRAELITES AND LATER HE WROTE HIS RULES FOR THE PEOPLE ON NEW STONE TABLETS.

Grasshopper Complex

NUMBERS 13–14

THE ISRAELITES LEFT MOUNT SINAI AND TRAVELED ON THROUGH THE DESERT.

SET UP CAMP HERE, ON THE BORDER OF CANAAN, THE LAND GOD SAID HE WILL GIVE TO US.

THE OTHER TEN SPIES BEGAN SPREADING LIES ABOUT THE LAND . . .

LISTEN TO US. THE PEOPLE ARE GIANTS.

WE'VE NEVER SEEN MEN SO BIG.

WE FELT LIKE GRASSHOPPERS BESIDE THEM—AND THAT'S PROBABLY HOW WE LOOKED!

GOD BECAME ANGRY WHEN THE PEOPLE LISTENED TO THE TEN SPIES INSTEAD OF TO JOSHUA AND CALEB.

THE TEN SPIES WHO REFUSED TO TRUST GOD DIED BECAUSE THEY TURNED THE PEOPLE AWAY FROM GOD'S PLAN. TO THE REST OF ISRAEL, GOD SAID . . .

YOU WILL ALL DIE HERE IN THIS WILDERNESS. BECAUSE YOU COMPLAINED AGAINST ME, NONE OF YOU WHO ARE TWENTY YEARS OLD OR OLDER AND WERE COUNTED IN THE CENSUS WILL ENTER THE LAND I SWORE TO GIVE YOU.

THE ONLY EXCEPTIONS WILL BE CALEB SON OF JEPHUNNEH AND JOSHUA SON OF NUN. BECAUSE THE MEN WHO EXPLORED THE LAND WERE THERE FOR FORTY DAYS, YOU MUST WANDER IN THE WILDERNESS FOR FORTY YEARS— A YEAR FOR EACH DAY—SUFFERING THE CONSEQUENCES OF YOUR SINS.

Unexpected Help

JOSHUA 2

RAHAB WENT BACK UP TO THE ROOF.

I KNOW ABOUT YOUR GOD. HE IS GOING TO GIVE YOU THIS LAND. EVERYONE IN MY COUNTRY IS DEATHLY AFRAID OF YOU. WE'VE HEARD ABOUT WHAT GOD HAS DONE FOR YOU, AND WE KNOW WE DON'T STAND A CHANCE AGAINST YOU.

PROMISE THAT YOU WILL PROTECT ME AND MY FAMILY BECAUSE I HAVE PROTECTED YOU.

IT'S A DEAL.

WE PLEDGE OUR LIVES FOR YOUR LIVES.

She Loves Me, She Loves Me Not

JUDGES 16:1-22

SAMSON HAD SOME TOUGH TIMES WITH THE PHILISTINES—BATTLES WHERE HE KILLED MANY PHILISTINE SOLDIERS SINGLE-HANDEDLY. FOR THE PAST TWENTY YEARS, SAMSON HAD SERVED AS A JUDGE FOR THE ISRAELITE PEOPLE. HE WAS STRONGER THAN ANY MAN ALIVE, BUT THE PHILISTINES HATED HIM.

That's All, Folks!

JUDGES 16:21-31

SAMSON WAS BOUND
WITH CHAINS AND LED
THROUGH GAZA.
CROWDS LINED THE
STREETS TO MAKE FUN
OF HIM.

LOOK AT BIG,
STRONG SAMSON NOW.
HE'S SO WEAK HE CAN'T
HURT A FLY!

THE PHILISTINES GOUGED OUT SAMSON'S EYES
AND PUT HIM TO WORK GRINDING GRAIN IN THE
PRISON. THEY DIDN'T NOTICE WHEN HIS HAIR
BEGAN TO GROW LONG AGAIN.

Will the Real Mother Please Speak Up?

1 KINGS 3; 2 CHRONICLES 1:3-12

LATER, DAVID BECAME KING OF ISRAEL, A POSITION HE HELD UNTIL HIS DEATH. DAVID'S SON, SOLOMON, BECAME KING AFTER DAVID DIED. SOLOMON WAS YOUNG AND INEXPERIENCED, BUT HE HAD A GREAT DESIRE TO SERVE GOD. ONE NIGHT SOLOMON HAD A STRANGE DREAM.

WHAT DO YOU WANT? ASK, AND I WILL GIVE IT TO YOU!

O GOD, YOU SHOWED GREAT LOVE TO MY FATHER, DAVID. AND EVEN THOUGH I'M YOUNG AND INEXPERIENCED, YOU'VE MADE ME KING IN HIS PLACE. GIVE ME A HEART THAT LISTENS SO THAT I CAN JUDGE YOUR PEOPLE AND TELL THE DIFFERENCE BETWEEN GOOD AND EVIL.

THE LORD WAS PLEASED THAT SOLOMON ASKED FOR A WISE HEART.

BECAUSE YOU HAVE ASKED FOR WISDOM IN GOVERNING MY PEOPLE AND HAVE NOT ASKED FOR A LONG LIFE OR RICHES FOR YOURSELF OR THE DEATH OF YOUR ENEMIES, I WILL GIVE YOU WHAT YOU ASKED FOR! I WILL GIVE YOU A WISE AND UNDERSTANDING MIND SUCH AS NO ONE ELSE HAS EVER HAD OR EVER WILL HAVE!

AND I WILL ALSO GIVE YOU WHAT YOU DID NOT ASK FOR—RICHES AND HONOR! NO OTHER KING IN ALL THE WORLD WILL BE COMPARED TO YOU FOR THE REST OF YOUR LIFE!

King of the Mountain

1 KINGS 18:16-40

THE DROUGHT DRAGGED ON FOR SEVERAL MONTHS. FINALLY ELIJAH WENT TO SEE KING AHAB.

YOU TROUBLEMAKER! LOOK AT THE PROBLEMS YOU'VE CAUSED ISRAEL.

NONE OF THIS IS MY FAULT! THESE PROBLEMS REST ON YOUR SHOULDERS BECAUSE YOU DISOBEYED GOD AND WORSHIPED BAAL.

CALL TOGETHER THE WHOLE NATION OF ISRAEL AND ALL THE PROPHETS OF BAAL. MEET ME ON MT. CARMEL, AND WE'LL SETTLE THIS ONCE AND FOR ALL.

AHAB CALLED EVERYONE TOGETHER AND SOON A HUGE CROWD OF PEOPLE, INCLUDING THE 450 PROPHETS OF BAAL, GATHERED ON MT. CARMEL. ELIJAH STOOD UP IN FRONT OF EVERYONE.

HOW LONG WILL YOU TRY TO HAVE IT BOTH WAYS? IF THE LORD IS GOD, FOLLOW HIM. IF BAAL IS GOD, THEN FOLLOW HIM.

MAKE UP YOUR MINDS!

NO ONE SAID A WORD.

Outstanding Debt

2 KINGS 4:1-7

ELISHA WAS CHOSEN TO BE GOD'S PROPHET AFTER ELIJAH WAS TAKEN TO HEAVEN. ELISHA KEPT BUSY TEACHING ABOUT GOD, HELPING GOD'S PEOPLE, AND DEALING WITH KINGS WHO DISHONORED GOD.

ONE DAY A WOMAN WHOSE HUSBAND HAD BEEN A DISCIPLE OF GOD'S PROPHETS CAME TO ELISHA . . .

MY HUSBAND IS DEAD. BUT A MAN SHOWED UP AT MY HOUSE SAYING THAT MY HUSBAND OWED HIM MONEY. HE IS DEMANDING THAT I PAY HIM, BUT I DON'T HAVE ANYTHING!

THE MAN IS COMING BACK. HE SAYS HE WILL TAKE MY TWO CHILDREN AS HIS PAYMENT. HE WILL MAKE THEM SLAVES.

PLEASE HELP ME—MY CHILDREN ARE ALL I HAVE LEFT!

I'LL DO WHAT I CAN. TELL ME WHAT YOU HAVE IN YOUR HOUSE THAT MIGHT BE USEFUL.

I HAVE NOTHING . . .

EXCEPT A JAR OF OLIVE OIL.

Faith's Reward

2 KINGS 4:8-37

A RICH WOMAN LIVED IN SHUNEM, A TOWN ELISHA OFTEN PASSED THROUGH ON HIS TRAVELS. SHE HAD INVITED ELISHA TO STOP AT HER HOUSE WHENEVER HE WAS IN THE AREA, SO HE WOULD STOP BY TO EAT.

YOU KNOW, ELISHA IS A HOLY MAN OF GOD, AND HE'S IN TOWN SO OFTEN—WHY DON'T WE JUST BUILD A SMALL ROOM FOR HIM TO STAY IN? WE HAVE THE SPACE AND HE WOULD ONLY NEED A BED, TABLE, CHAIR, AND LAMP.

THE WOMAN AND HER HUSBAND BUILT A ROOM FOR ELISHA AND HE STAYED WITH THEM OFTEN.

GEHAZI, SPEAK TO THE SHUNEMITE WOMAN FOR ME. ASK HER IF THERE IS ANYTHING WE CAN DO FOR HER.

BUT WHEN SHE GOT CLOSE TO ELISHA, SHE FELL DOWN AND GRABBED HIS FEET. GEHAZI STARTED TO PULL HER AWAY, BUT ELISHA STOPPED HIM.

LEAVE HER ALONE. SHE IS VERY UPSET, BUT I DON'T KNOW WHY. JUST WAIT.

I DIDN'T ASK YOU FOR A SON, DID I? IN FACT, I SAID, DON'T GET MY HOPES UP!

GEHAZI, GET MY SHEPHERD'S STAFF AND HURRY TO SHUNEM. DON'T STOP TO TALK TO ANYONE! WHEN YOU GET THERE, LAY MY STAFF ON THE BOY'S FACE!

I'M NOT LEAVING HERE WITHOUT YOU, ELISHA!

ELISHA GOT UP AND WENT WITH THE GRIEF-STRICKEN MOTHER.

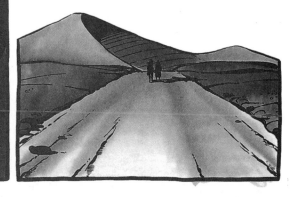

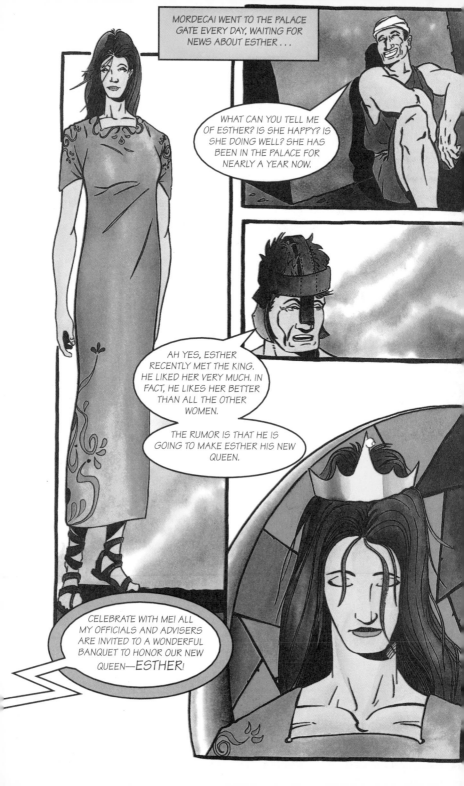

Read it and Weep

KING BELSHAZZAR OF BABYLON THREW A HUGE BANQUET FOR 1,000 IMPORTANT PEOPLE.

DANIEL 5

BRING THE GOLD AND SILVER CUPS THAT MY GRANDFATHER NEBUCHADNEZZAR TOOK FROM THE JEW'S TEMPLE. WE'LL SEE HOW OUR FINE WINE TASTES FROM HOLY CUPS!

HAA HAA HAA!

AS THE KING AND HIS GUESTS WERE DRINKING FROM THE GOLD AND SILVER CUPS . . .

AAAHHHH!!! THERE'S A HAND WITH NO BODY ATTACHED TO IT AND IT'S WRITING SOMETHING ON THE WALL!

Go Where and Preach What?

JONAH 1

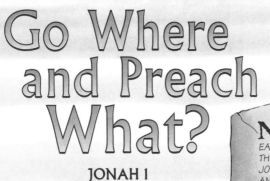

NINEVEH WAS ONE OF THE MOST EVIL CITIES ON EARTH. EVEN SO, GOD LOVED THE PEOPLE THERE. HE TOLD JONAH TO GO TO NINEVEH AND TO TELL THE PEOPLE TO TURN AWAY FROM THEIR SIN AND FOLLOW GOD.

GET UP AND GO TO THE GREAT CITY OF NINEVEH! ANNOUNCE MY JUDGMENT AGAINST IT BECAUSE I HAVE SEEN HOW WICKED ITS PEOPLE ARE.

NINEVEH? WHO CARES ABOUT THAT ROTTEN CITY? I DON'T CARE IF EVERYONE THERE DIES.

JONAH'S OPINION DIDN'T CHANGE GOD'S MIND. HE STILL WANTED JONAH TO PREACH IN NINEVEH. INSTEAD OF OBEYING GOD, JONAH RAN AWAY.

WHERE'S THIS SHIP HEADED?

TARSHISH.

"GREAT. HERE'S THE MONEY FOR MY FARE. I'M GOING BELOW FOR A NAP. WAKE ME WHEN WE GET TO TARSHISH."

THAT'S SETTLED. THE LAST PLACE I WANT TO GO IS NINEVEH, SO I'LL JUST HIDE DOWN HERE. BY THE TIME GOD FINDS OUT I DIDN'T GO TO NINEVEH, I'LL BE LOST IN THE CROWDS OF TARSHISH.

BUT AS THE SHIP SET OUT TOWARD TARSHISH . . .

CAPTAIN, THE WIND IS GETTING STRONGER, AND WE'RE TAKING ON SOME WATER.

ANY MINUTE OUR SHIP IS GOING TO BE NOTHING BUT SPLINTERS IN THE WATER.

EVERYONE PRAY TO THE SEA GODS—MAYBE THEY WILL HELP US.

YOU MEN COME WITH ME. WE'LL THROW SOME OF THE CARGO OVERBOARD. MAYBE IT'LL HELP IF THE SHIP IS LIGHTER.

I'M GOING TO WAKE JONAH AND SEE IF HE CAN HELP.

HOW CAN YOU SLEEP? HAVEN'T YOU NOTICED THAT WE'RE IN SERIOUS TROUBLE HERE? GET UP! IF YOU HAVE A GOD, PRAY TO HIM!

The New Testament

A Most Awesome Night

LUKE 2:1-20

THE ANGEL GABRIEL CAME TO NAZARETH AND INFORMED MARY AND JOSEPH THAT MARY WOULD SOON HAVE A BABY BOY—THE SON OF GOD. THEY WERE TO NAME HIM JESUS. A SHORT WHILE LATER . . .

THE GOVERNOR OF OUR LAND WANTS TO COUNT HOW MANY PEOPLE LIVE HERE. HE HAS ORDERED THAT WE ALL MUST GO TO THE CITIES WHERE OUR ANCESTORS LIVED TO REGISTER.

THAT MEANS WE HAVE TO TRAVEL ALL THE WAY TO BETHLEHEM. I CAN'T ASK YOU TO MAKE THE TRIP—YOUR BABY IS DUE ANY DAY NOW.

DON'T WORRY ABOUT ME JOSEPH, I'LL BE ALRIGHT. I'M COMING WITH YOU.

SO THE YOUNG COUPLE SET OFF FOR BETHLEHEM WHERE JOSEPH'S LONG AGO RELATIVE, KING DAVID, HAD LIVED.

THE TRIP TOOK THEM SEVERAL DAYS BECAUSE MARY HAD TO STOP OFTEN TO REST.

The First Birthday Gifts
MATTHEW 2:1-12
ON A SPECIAL NIGHT IN BETHLEHEM, GOD'S SON JESUS WAS BORN. MARY LAID HER SWEET BABY IN A MANGER TO SLEEP AS ANGELS ANNOUNCED JESUS' BIRTH TO SHEPHERDS IN THE FIELD OUTSIDE TOWN. THE VERY NIGHT THAT JESUS WAS BORN, A STRANGE THING HAPPENED HUNDREDS OF MILES FROM BETHLEHEM.
LOOK! THERE'S A NEW STAR IN THE SKY TONIGHT. WHAT DOES THAT MEAN?
I REMEMBER HEARING THAT THE APPEARANCE OF A NEW STAR MEANS THAT THE TRUE KING OF THE JEWS HAS BEEN BORN.

THE WISE MEN PACKED GIFTS FOR THE NEW KING AND BEGAN FOLLOWING THE STAR AS IT MOVED SLOWLY THROUGH THE SKY TOWARD BETHLEHEM.
AFTER TRAVELING A LONG TIME, THEY ARRIVED IN JERUSALEM.

An Unexpected Trip

MATTHEW 2:13-18

THE WISE MEN FOLLOWED THE STAR TO FIND THE CHILD BORN TO BE KING OF THE JEWS. AFTER THEY GAVE HIM GIFTS, THEY WERE WARNED IN A DREAM TO RETURN HOME BY A DIFFERENT ROUTE. ABOUT THAT TIME GOD SPOKE TO SOMEONE ELSE IN A DREAM . . .

GET UP AND FLEE TO EGYPT WITH THE CHILD AND HIS MOTHER. STAY THERE UNTIL I TELL YOU TO RETURN, BECAUSE HEROD IS GOING TO TRY TO KILL THE CHILD.

Face on a Milk Carton

LUKE 2:41-52

MARY AND JOSEPH RETURNED TO NAZARETH AFTER KING HEROD DIED. THEY CARED FOR YOUNG JESUS AND TAUGHT HIM AS THEY DID THEIR OTHER CHILDREN.

IT'S TIME TO TRAVEL TO JERUSALEM FOR THE PASSOVER FESTIVAL. JESUS, YOU'RE 12 YEARS OLD NOW, OLD ENOUGH TO UNDERSTAND WHAT IT'S ALL ABOUT.

THE SMALL FAMILY, ALONG WITH RELATIVES AND FRIENDS OBSERVED THE TRADITIONAL PASSOVER FEAST. WHEN THE CELEBRATION WAS OVER, THEY ALL HEADED FOR HOME.

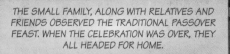

NO, I HAVEN'T SEEN HIM SINCE WE LEFT JERUSALEM EARLY THIS MORNING.

HAVE YOU SEEN JESUS?

MARY AND JOSEPH SEARCHED ALL THROUGH THE CROWD OF PEOPLE WITH WHOM THEY WERE TRAVELING. THEY COULDN'T FIND JESUS ANYWHERE.

HE'S PROBABLY WALKING WITH SOME OF THE OTHER CHILDREN BACK THERE.

JOSEPH, WHERE IS HE? WHERE IS JESUS?

HE MUST HAVE STAYED BEHIND IN JERUSALEM.

THEN WE HAVE TO GO BACK THERE NOW. WE HAVE TO FIND HIM!

What a Wedding Gift

JOHN 2:1-11

JESUS CHOSE THE 12 MEN WHO WOULD BE HIS CLOSEST FOLLOWERS AND STUDENTS. THEY BEGAN TRAVELING THROUGH GALILEE AND THEY REACHED THE SMALL TOWN OF CANA.

JESUS, MY FRIEND. I'M GETTING MARRIED TODAY. COME TO THE PARTY AND BRING YOUR FRIENDS ALONG!

WHAT A BIG CELEBRATION!

YES, SO MANY PEOPLE ARE HERE!

JESUS, ISN'T THAT YOUR MOTHER OVER THERE?

MARY CAME OVER TO JESUS.

THIS HAS BEEN A MAGNIFICENT PARTY, BUT THERE'S A PROBLEM. THE HOST HAS RUN OUT OF WINE TO SERVE THE GUESTS. THAT'S A VERY BAD THING FOR HIM, YOU KNOW. CAN'T YOU HELP OUR FRIEND?

Spring Cleaning

JOHN 2:13-22

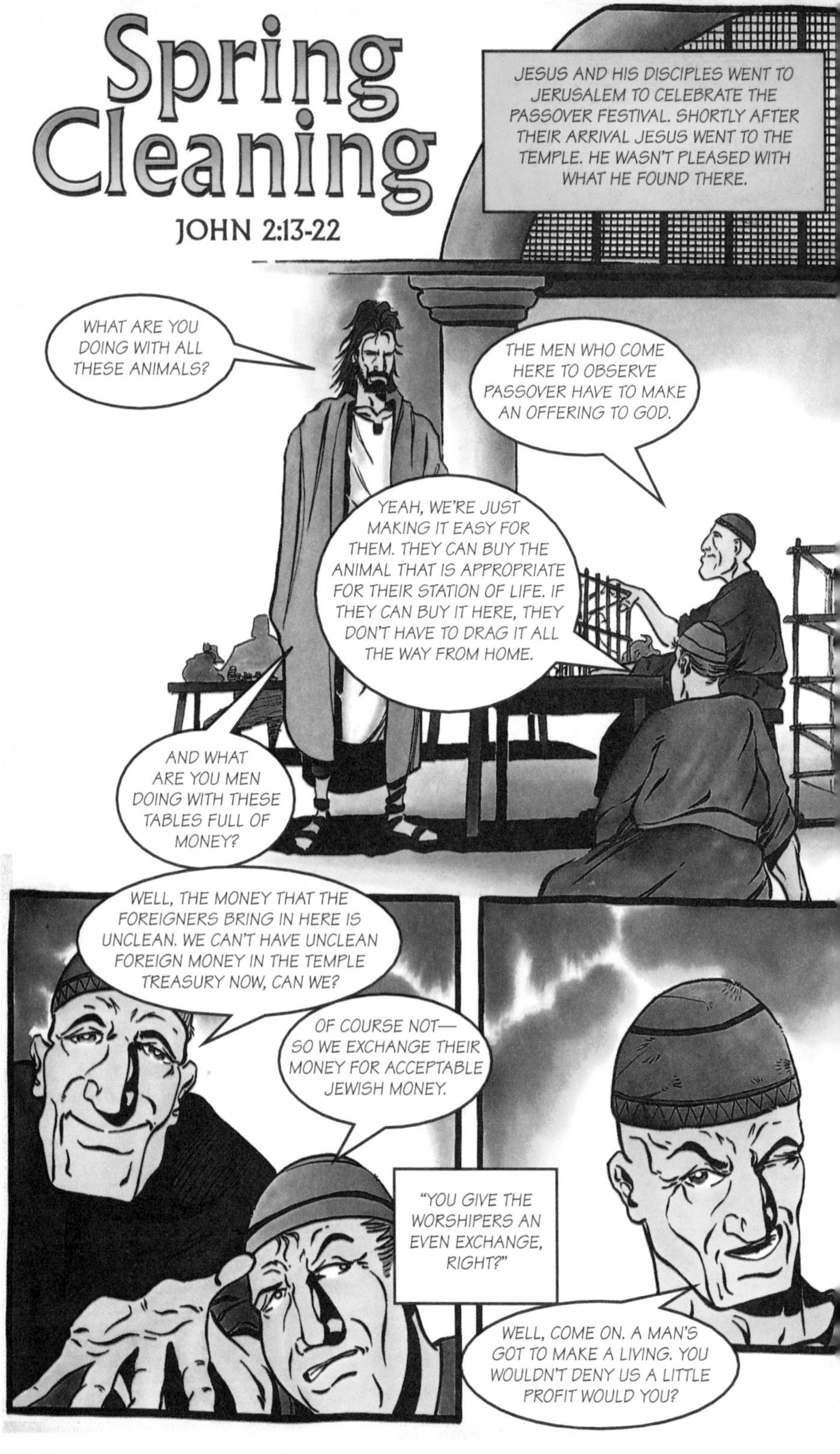

The Fish that Get Didn't Away

LUKE 5:1-11

I KNOW, IF HE BACKS UP ANYMORE, HE WILL BE IN THE WATER!

COME ON, LET'S GET OUR NETS CLEANED UP SO WE CAN GO HOME AND GET SOME SLEEP.

A FEW MINUTES LATER SIMON PETER LOOKED UP TO SEE JESUS CLIMBING INTO HIS BOAT.

SO, YOUR AUDIENCE PUSHED YOU RIGHT OFF THE SHORE, EH?

WOULD YOU PUSH THE BOAT OUT INTO THE WATER A LITTLE WAY SO I CAN CONTINUE TEACHING?

SIMON PUSHED THE BOAT AWAY FROM SHORE, AND JESUS TAUGHT THE CROWD A LITTLE WHILE LONGER. WHEN HE FINISHED, HE TURNED HIS ATTENTION TO SIMON PETER.

NOW GO OUT WHERE IT IS DEEPER AND LET DOWN YOUR NETS, AND YOU WILL CATCH MANY FISH.

LOOK, TEACHER, MY CREW AND I WORKED HARD ALL NIGHT, AND HOW MANY FISH DID WE CATCH? EXACTLY ZERO. WE'RE TIRED, AND WE WANT TO GO HOME AND REST.

On the Road with Jesus

MATTHEW 4:23-25;
MARK 1:29-39;
LUKE 4:38-44

JESUS TRAVELED AND TAUGHT FROM CAPERNAUM TO NAZARETH. ONE TIME IN CAPERNAUM HE WENT TO SIMON'S HOUSE . . .

JESUS, SIMON'S MOTHER-IN-LAW HAS A TERRIBLE FEVER. SHE'S SO SICK THAT SHE CAN'T GET OUT OF BED.

WAIT, YOU SHOULDN'T GO IN THERE. YOU MIGHT CATCH HER FEVER.

JESUS WALKED RIGHT UP TO THE WOMAN'S BED AND STRETCHED HIS HAND OUT TOWARD HER.

WHAT'S HE DOING? SHE'S TOO SICK TO EVEN OPEN HER EYES.

NO LOOK, HER EYES ARE OPEN AND SHE'S TAKING HIS HAND.

I FEEL FINE NOW. LET ME COOK DINNER FOR ALL OF YOU.

THE NEXT MORNING . . .

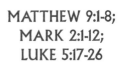

MATTHEW 9:1-8;
MARK 2:1-12;
LUKE 5:17-26

Hope it Doesn't Rain!

JESUS TRAVELED AROUND, TEACHING ABOUT GOD. WHEN HE CAME BACK TO CAPERNAUM . . .

HAVE YOU HEARD? JESUS IS BACK!

CALL YOUR FRIENDS AND FAMILY, JESUS IS BACK! HE'S GOING TO TEACH!

BEFORE LONG THE LITTLE HOUSE WHERE HE WAS STAYING WAS JAMMED WITH PEOPLE.

LET ME IN, I WANT TO HEAR WHAT HE'S TEACHING ABOUT!

STOP PUSHING! THERE'S NOT ROOM FOR EVEN ONE MORE BODY, SO PUSHING WON'T HELP.

SOME PHARISEES AND EXPERTS IN MOSES' TEACHINGS GOT TO THE HOUSE EARLY AND HAD FRONT ROW SEATS.

LISTEN TO EVERY WORD JESUS SAYS. WE'LL GET THE PROOF WE NEED THAT HE'S A FAKE WHO DISHONORS GOD.

"SIMON (WHOM I WILL CALL PETER)"

"JAMES AND JOHN (WHOM I'VE NICKNAMED "THUNDERBOLTS")"

"ANDREW"

"PHILIP"

"BARTHOLOMEW"

"MATTHEW"

"THOMAS"

"JAMES"

Just Say the Word

MATTHEW 8:5-13;
LUKE 7:1-10

ONE TIME JESUS CAME TO CAPERNAUM WITH HIS FRIENDS. AN OFFICER FROM THE ROMAN ARMY RUSHED UP AND PUSHED HIS WAY THROUGH THE CROWD SURROUNDING JESUS . . .

SIR, CAN I TALK TO YOU? PLEASE LISTEN TO ME! MY MOST TREASURED SERVANT HAS BECOME PARALYZED. HE'S BACK AT MY HOUSE. HE CAN'T MOVE, AND HE'S IN TERRIBLE PAIN. PLEASE, WILL YOU HELP HIM?

THE CROWD AROUND JESUS GREW QUIET AS JESUS LOOKED AT THE ARMY OFFICER. HE UNDERSTOOD THE MAN'S WORRY AND PAIN.

I WILL COME AND HEAL HIM.

THEN JESUS STARTED WALKING TOWARD THE MAN'S HOME WITH THE HUGE CROWD FOLLOWING ALONG.

E-I-E-I Splash!
MATTHEW 8:28-34; MARK 5:1-20; LUKE 8:26-39
THE SAME DAY THAT JESUS STOPPED THE STORM, HIS BOAT ARRIVED IN GERASENES, ACROSS THE SEA FROM GALILEE.
HEY YOU! JESUS! WHAT ARE YOU DOING HERE?
WHO IS THAT?
AH, HE'S A CRAZY MAN THAT LIVES IN THE CEMETERY UP THERE.
STAY AWAY FROM HIM, HE'S DANGEROUS. IN FACT, MOST PEOPLE DON'T EVEN TRAVEL DOWN THIS ROAD MUCH ANYMORE BECAUSE YOU NEVER KNOW WHAT HE'S GOING TO DO!
I DON'T THINK HE'S CRAZY—LOOK AT HOW HE'S ACTING AROUND JESUS. I THINK HE'S GOT DEMONS LIVING IN HIM!
YEAH, I'VE HEARD THEY ONCE HAD HIM CHAINED HAND AND FOOT, BUT HE BROKE THE CHAINS.
HE SITS UP BY THE TOMBS AND SCREAMS AND CUTS HIMSELF WITH ROCKS.

WATCH OUT! THE PIGS ARE STAMPEDING!

GET OUT OF THE WAY. WE'RE GOING TO BE KILLED.

"LOOK, THE PIGS RAN STRAIGHT DOWN THE CLIFF AND INTO THE SEA. ALL 2,000 OF THEM DROWNED."

THE MEN WHO TOOK CARE OF THE PIGS RAN INTO TOWN AND TOLD EVERYTHING THAT HAD HAPPENED. THE TOWNSPEOPLE CAME RUNNING OUT TO WHERE JESUS WAS.

WHO'S THAT MAN SITTING BESIDE THE TEACHER?

HEY, IT'S THE CRAZY MAN!

NAH, IT CAN'T BE, THAT MAN IS WEARING CLOTHES AND CARRYING ON A NORMAL CONVERSATION.

WHAT'S GOING ON HERE? I FEEL KIND OF SPOOKY ABOUT ALL THIS.

Power Surge

A NOISY CROWD FILLED THE HOUSE. PEOPLE WAILED AND MOANED AND CRIED.

STOP THE WEEPING! SHE ISN'T DEAD; SHE IS ONLY ASLEEP.

HA! WHAT KIND OF FOOL IS HE? WE KNOW WHEN A PERSON IS DEAD.

DEAD IS DEAD! WHAT CAN THE "HEALER" DO NOW?

LEAVE!

JESUS TOOK THE CHILD'S MOTHER AND FATHER AND HIS THREE FRIENDS AND WENT TO THE LITTLE GIRL'S BEDSIDE. AS HE TOOK HER HAND HE SAID:

GET UP, MY CHILD!

THE GRIEVING PARENTS HELD THEIR BREATH AND AT ONCE,

SHE'S GETTING UP!

I CAN'T BELIEVE IT. ONLY A MOMENT AGO MY BABY WAS DEAD, BUT NOW SHE'S WALKING AROUND AND TALKING!

JESUS TOLD THEM TO GET THEIR DAUGHTER SOMETHING TO EAT, AND HE ORDERED THEM NOT TO TELL ANYONE WHAT HAD JUST HAPPENED.

Hold the Pickle Please!

MATTHEW 14:13-21;
MARK 6:30-44;
LUKE 9:10-17;
JOHN 6:1-14

JESUS AND HIS DISCIPLES WENT TO BETHSAIDA TO HAVE SOME TIME ALONE TOGETHER.

THIS CROWD FOLLOWS US EVERYWHERE. WHY CAN'T WE JUST BE ALONE FOR AWHILE?

CAN YOU BLAME THEM? THEY'VE HEARD ABOUT ALL THE PEOPLE JESUS HAS HEALED. THE PEOPLE HAVE BROUGHT THOSE THEY LOVE WHO ARE SICK OR LAME.

YES, AND SOME OF THEM ARE JUST CURIOUS ABOUT WHO JESUS IS.

JESUS WANTED TIME ALONE, BUT WHEN HE SAW THE CROWD WAITING FOR HIM TO TEACH THEM, HE FELT SORRY FOR THEM AND BEGAN TO TEACH.

While Strollin'
on the Sea One Day

MATTHEW 14:22-33;
MARK 6:47-52;
JOHN 6:16-21

AFTER JESUS FED THE 5,000 PEOPLE, HE SENT HIS DISCIPLES BACK TO CAPERNAUM. HE WENT UP INTO THE MOUNTAINS ALONE TO PRAY. MEANWHILE THE DISCIPLES WERE HAVING PROBLEMS . . .

THE WAVES ARE GETTING HIGHER AND HIGHER.

THEY'RE TOSSING THIS BOAT AROUND LIKE IT'S A PIECE OF DRIFTWOOD!

I DON'T WANT TO SCARE YOU GUYS, BUT I WAS A FISHERMAN FOR YEARS—AND I'M TELLING YOU WE'RE IN SERIOUS TROUBLE HERE!

HOW DID HE GIVE YOU SIGHT? WHAT DID HE DO?

I ALREADY TOLD YOU ONCE, AND YOU DIDN'T LISTEN TO ME. WHY DO YOU WANT TO HEAR THE STORY AGAIN? ARE YOU THINKING OF BECOMING JESUS' DISCIPLES?

YOU FOOL! YOU MAY BE HIS DISCIPLE, BUT WE'RE MOSES' DISCIPLES. WE KNOW THAT GOD SPOKE TO MOSES—BUT WE DON'T KNOW WHERE THIS JESUS CAME FROM!

AMAZING! YOU DON'T KNOW WHERE HE'S FROM, BUT HE WAS ABLE TO GIVE ME SIGHT. DOES GOD LISTEN TO SINNERS? NO, HE LISTENS TO PEOPLE WHO LOVE AND FOLLOW HIM! IF JESUS WERE NOT FROM GOD, HE COULDN'T DO ANYTHING LIKE THIS!

YOU LOUSY SINNER! DO YOU THINK YOU KNOW MORE THAN WE DO? GET OUT OF THE SYNAGOGUE AND DON'T EVER DARE TO COME IN HERE AGAIN!

Lovin' Your Neighbor

LUKE 10:25-37

A MAN WHO WAS AN EXPERT IN MOSES' TEACHINGS WAS LISTENING TO JESUS TEACH. HE ASKED JESUS A QUESTION, HOPING HE COULD TRICK HIM.

WHAT MUST I DO TO GET ETERNAL LIFE?

WHAT DOES THE LAW OF MOSES SAY? HOW DO YOU READ IT?

IT SAYS TO LOVE THE LORD YOUR GOD WITH ALL YOUR HEART, WITH ALL YOUR SOUL, WITH ALL YOUR STRENGTH, AND WITH ALL YOUR MIND. AND TO LOVE YOUR NEIGHBOR AS YOU LOVE YOURSELF.

RIGHT! DO THIS AND YOU WILL LIVE.

"THEN A DESPISED SAMARITAN CAME ALONG, AND WHEN HE SAW THE MAN, HE FELT DEEP PITY. KNEELING BESIDE HIM, THE SAMARITAN SOOTHED HIS WOUNDS WITH MEDICINE AND BANDAGED THEM. THEN HE PUT THE MAN ON HIS OWN DONKEY AND TOOK HIM TO AN INN, WHERE HE TOOK CARE OF HIM."

"THE NEXT DAY HE HANDED THE INNKEEPER TWO PIECES OF SILVER AND TOLD HIM TO TAKE CARE OF THE MAN."

IF HIS BILL RUNS HIGHER THAN THAT, I'LL PAY THE DIFFERENCE THE NEXT TIME I AM HERE.

Happy Birthday . . . Again

JOHN 11:1-44

MARY, HER SISTER MARTHA, AND THEIR BROTHER LAZARUS WERE GOOD FRIENDS OF JESUS. SO WHEN LAZARUS BECAME DEATHLY ILL, HIS SISTERS KNEW EXACTLY WHAT TO DO . . .

MARY AND MARTHA SENT ME TO GET YOU. LAZARUS IS REALLY SICK. IN FACT, THEY'RE AFRAID HE MIGHT DIE!

HUF HEF

"LAZARUS'S SICKNESS WILL NOT END IN DEATH. NO, IT IS FOR THE GLORY OF GOD. I, THE SON OF GOD, WILL RECEIVE GLORY FROM THIS."

JESUS CARED A LOT ABOUT MARY, MARTHA, AND LAZARUS, BUT THIS NEWS DIDN'T SEEM TO UPSET HIM.

THE MESSENGER SAID LAZARUS IS VERY SICK. WHY ISN'T JESUS GOING TO SEE HIM?

I DON'T KNOW, IT'S BEEN TWO DAYS SINCE THE MESSENGER CAME, AND JESUS HASN'T SAID ANYTHING ABOUT GOING TO BETHANY.

BUT ON THAT VERY DAY, JESUS SAID:

LET'S GO TO JUDEA AGAIN.

JUDEA!? THE LAST TIME WE WERE THERE THE JEWS WANTED TO STONE YOU TO DEATH.

WHY WOULD YOU WANT TO GO BACK THERE?

OUR FRIEND LAZARUS HAS FALLEN ASLEEP, BUT NOW I WILL GO AND WAKE HIM.

You Don't Have to Tell Me Twice!

LUKE 19:1-10

JESUS WAS TRAVELING THROUGH JERICHO, AND AS USUAL, A HUGE CROWD GATHERED TO SEE HIM.

WHY IS THIS CROWD HERE TODAY?

THEY'RE ALL HERE TO SEE JESUS, THE TEACHER.

OH, I'VE HEARD OF HIM. I'D LIKE TO SEE HIM, TOO.

WELL, YOU'D BETTER HURRY. THE PATH IS ALREADY LINED ON BOTH SIDES.

WELL, THEY'LL LET ME THROUGH. AFTER ALL, I'M ZACCHAEUS, HEAD OF THE TAX COLLECTORS!

TO ZACCHAEUS' SURPRISE THOUGH, THE PEOPLE WOULDN'T LET HIM THROUGH.

Making an Entrance

MATTHEW 21:1-9; MARK 11:1-11; LUKE 19:29-44; JOHN 12:12-19

JESUS AND HIS DISCIPLES WERE ON THEIR WAY TO JERUSALEM TO CELEBRATE THE PASSOVER. BEFORE THEY REACHED THE CITY, JESUS STOPPED AND SENT TWO DISCIPLES ON AN ERRAND.

"GO INTO THAT VILLAGE OVER THERE, AND AS YOU ENTER IT, YOU WILL SEE A COLT TIED THERE THAT HAS NEVER BEEN RIDDEN. UNTIE IT AND BRING IT HERE. IF ANYONE ASKS WHAT YOU ARE DOING, JUST SAY, 'THE LORD NEEDS IT.' "

THERE—SEE THAT YOUNG DONKEY? THAT MUST BE THE ONE JESUS WAS TALKING ABOUT.

OK, LET'S TAKE IT.

The Beginning of the End

MATTHEW 26:17-30; MARK 14:12-26; LUKE 22:7-20

IT WAS NEARLY TIME TO CELEBRATE THE PASSOVER FEAST, SO JESUS' DISCIPLES CAME TO HIM FOR INSTRUCTIONS ...

"WHERE DO YOU WANT US TO PREPARE THE PASSOVER MEAL FOR YOU?"

JESUS LOOKED TOWARD JERUSALEM.

"AS SOON AS YOU ENTER JERUSALEM, A MAN CARRYING A PITCHER OF WATER WILL MEET YOU. FOLLOW HIM. AT THE HOUSE HE ENTERS, SAY TO THE OWNER, 'THE TEACHER ASKS, WHERE IS THE GUEST ROOM WHERE I CAN EAT THE PASSOVER MEAL WITH MY DISCIPLES?' HE WILL TAKE YOU UPSTAIRS TO A LARGE ROOM THAT IS ALREADY SET UP. THAT IS THE PLACE. GO AHEAD AND PREPARE OUR SUPPER THERE."

I DON'T UNDERSTAND THIS, BUT I TRUST JESUS.

ME TOO, I'M WILLING TO DO WHATEVER HE ASKS.

SO THE TWO MEN PREPARED THE PASSOVER MEAL ACCORDING TO JEWISH TRADITION.

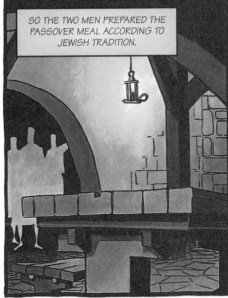

Terror in the Night

MATTHEW 26:36-75;
MARK 14:32-72;
LUKE 22:39-62;
JOHN 18:2-27

JESUS AND HIS DISCIPLES LEFT THE UPSTAIRS ROOM WHERE THEY ATE THE PASSOVER MEAL, AND THEY WENT TO THE GARDEN OF GETHSEMANE. HE CALLED PETER, JAMES AND JOHN APART FROM THE GROUP. THE REST OF THE DISCIPLES WATCHED JESUS AND THE THREE MEN WALK AWAY.

BUT THEN JESUS HEARD THE NOISE OF A CROWD COMING THROUGH THE GARDEN.

UP, LET'S BE GOING. SEE, MY BETRAYER IS HERE!

IT'S JUDAS!

AND HE'S LEADING A CROWD OF ANGRY MEN.

THERE'S GONNA BE TROUBLE!

THE ONE I KISS IS THE MAN YOU WANT.

AS JESUS WAS SPEAKING . . .

COME ON, LET'S GET OUT OF HERE.

HAH! LOOK! EVERY ONE OF HIS DISCIPLES DESERTED HIM.

THEY ARRESTED JESUS AND TOOK HIM TO THE CHIEF PRIEST. PETER FOLLOWED A LITTLE WAY BEHIND AND STAYED IN THE COURTYARD TO WARM HIMSELF BY THE FIRE.

MEN OF THE COUNCIL, WE NEED A REASON TO HAVE THIS MAN EXECUTED! SURELY WITH ALL HE'S DONE WE CAN COME UP WITH ONE REASON!

WE'VE ARRESTED HIM. NOW WE NEED SOME TESTIMONY AGAINST HIM BEFORE WE CAN GO ANY FURTHER!

Guilty!
"CONDEMNED TO DEATH!"
THE PEOPLE WATCHING THE PROCEEDINGS ATTACKED JESUS, HITTING HIM WITH THEIR CLENCHED FISTS, SLAPPING HIM. SOME EVEN SPIT IN HIS FACE. EVEN THE GUARDS JOINED IN, HITTING AND SPITTING ON HIM.

MEANWHILE PETER WARMED HIMSELF BY THE FIRE IN THE COURTYARD. A WOMAN CAME UP TO HIM.

HEY, YOU'RE WITH THAT TEACHER, JESUS OF NAZARETH!

I DON'T KNOW HIM. I DON'T EVEN KNOW WHAT YOU'RE TALKING ABOUT.

PETER HEARD A ROOSTER CROW AS HE STOMPED AWAY.

BUT THE WOMAN WOULDN'T DROP IT . . .

THIS MAN IS ONE OF THEM!

NO I'M NOT. GET AWAY FROM ME!

I CAN TELL BY YOUR ACCENT THAT YOU'RE FROM GALILEE. YOU ARE ONE OF THEM!

I SWEAR TO YOU THAT I DON'T KNOW WHAT YOU'RE TALKING ABOUT!

PETER HEARD THE ROOSTER CROW AGAIN.

THEN HE REMEMBERED THAT JESUS HAD PREDICTED THAT BEFORE A ROOSTER CROWED TWICE, PETER WOULD SAY THREE TIMES THAT HE DIDN'T KNOW JESUS.

PETER DROPPED TO HIS KNEES AND CRIED BITTERLY.

The Darkest Day in History

PILATE GAVE THE JEWISH COUNCIL PERMISSION TO DO WHAT THEY WANTED WITH JESUS. SOLDIERS TOOK HIM INTO THE PALACE.

MATTHEW 27:27-66; MARK 15:16-47; LUKE 23:26-56; JOHN 19:1-3; 16-42

HEY, KING OF THE JEWS, PUT ON THIS ROYAL ROBE.

AND HERE'S A CROWN FOR YOUR ROYAL HEAD.

LONG LIVE THE KING! HA HA HA HA HA!

THE SOLDIERS CIRCLED AROUND JESUS, MAKING FUN OF HIM AND INSULTING HIM.

SOME OF THEM EVEN SPIT ON JESUS.

Friend Sightings

JESUS WAS MURDERED AND BURIED IN A STONE TOMB. THE DAY AFTER HIS DEATH, THE CHIEF PRIESTS AND PHARISEES BEGAN TO WORRY ABOUT SOMETHING . . .

MATTHEW 27:62–28:10; MARK 16:1-13;
LUKE 24:1-35; JOHN 20:1-18

YOU KNOW, THAT JEW PREDICTED THAT HE WOULD COME BACK TO LIFE THREE DAYS AFTER HIS DEATH.

PILATE, SECURE HIS TOMB SOMEHOW. MAKE SURE HIS FOLLOWERS DON'T STEAL HIS BODY AND THEN CLAIM THAT HE CAME BACK TO LIFE.

PILATE ORDERED THE TOMB SEALED AND POSTED GUARDS OUTSIDE IT.

AT DAYBREAK SUNDAY MORNING A GROUP OF HEARTBROKEN WOMEN SLOWLY WALKED TO JESUS' TOMB.

HOW ARE WE GOING TO ROLL THE BIG STONE AWAY SO WE CAN GET INSIDE TO PUT THESE SPICES ON JESUS' BODY?

MARY, LOOK! THE STONE HAS BEEN MOVED. THE TOMB IS OPEN!

WHAT'S GOING ON?

WHO ARE YOU?

DO NOT BE SO SURPRISED. YOU ARE LOOKING FOR JESUS, THE NAZARENE, WHO WAS CRUCIFIED. HE ISN'T HERE! HE HAS BEEN RAISED FROM THE DEAD. NOW GO AND GIVE THIS MESSAGE TO HIS DISCIPLES.

SOME OF THE WOMEN IMMEDIATELY RAN FOR TOWN. AS MARY MAGDALENE TURNED TO FOLLOW THEM, SHE SAW A MAN STANDING NEAR THE TOMB.

SIR, ARE YOU THE GARDENER? TELL ME WHAT YOU HAVE DONE WITH JESUS' BODY— PLEASE TELL ME.

MARY.

TEACHER!

DON'T CLING TO ME, FOR I HAVEN'T YET ASCENDED TO THE FATHER. BUT GO FIND MY BROTHERS AND TELL THEM THAT I AM ASCENDING TO MY FATHER AND YOUR FATHER, MY GOD AND YOUR GOD.

THEN THE STRANGER EXPLAINED EVERYTHING THE SCRIPTURES TAUGHT ABOUT THE MESSIAH.

THIS IS WHERE WE LIVE. WOULD YOU LIKE TO COME IN AND HAVE SOMETHING TO EAT WITH US?

THE MAN SAT DOWN TO EAT WITH THEM. AS HE BLESSED THE FOOD, THEY SUDDENLY KNEW WHO HE WAS.

JESUS, IT'S YOU!

AS QUICKLY AS THEY RECOGNIZED HIM, HE DISAPPEARED.

Flames of Rome
ACTS 2
FIFTY DAYS AFTER PASSOVER ALL THE BELIEVERS WERE TOGETHER IN ONE PLACE WHEN SOMETHING STRANGE BEGAN TO HAPPEN:
CHECK THE WINDOWS, IT SOUNDS LIKE A STORM IS BLOWING UP.
THE WINDOWS ARE CLOSED. BESIDES, THAT SOUND IS COMING FROM IN HERE! IT SOUNDS LIKE A TORNADO—INSIDE THIS ROOM!

What's Better than Money?

ACTS 3

EVERY DAY SOME MEN CARRIED THEIR CRIPPLED FRIEND TO THE BEAUTIFUL GATE NEAR THE TEMPLE IN JERUSALEM. HE SAT THERE AND BEGGED FOR MONEY FROM PEOPLE GOING IN AND OUT OF THE TEMPLE. ONE AFTERNOON PETER AND JOHN WERE WALKING THROUGH THE COURTYARD.

Chariot Chasing

ACTS 8:26-40

AN ANGEL OF GOD CAME TO PHILIP WITH A VERY IMPORTANT MESSAGE.

GO SOUTH DOWN THE DESERT ROAD THAT RUNS FROM JERUSALEM TO GAZA.

PHILIP DID WHAT THE ANGEL SAID.

PHILIP AND THE OFFICIAL STEPPED INTO THE WATER, AND PHILIP BAPTIZED HIM.

WHEN THEY CAME OUT OF THE WATER, THE SPIRIT OF THE LORD TOOK PHILIP AWAY, AND THE ETHIOPIAN DIDN'T SEE HIM AGAIN.

An Unexpected Career Change

ACTS 9:1-21, 28

SAUL HATED CHRISTIANS. HE HATED THEM SO MUCH THAT ALL HE WANTED TO DO WAS TO MAKE CHRISTIANS MISERABLE.

THROW THESE LOUSY CHRISTIANS IN PRISON. LET 'EM ROT THERE WHILE THEY THINK ABOUT THEIR PRECIOUS FAITH!

SIR, WILL YOU GIVE ME A LETTER OF INTRODUCTION TO THE SYNAGOGUE LEADERS IN DAMASCUS. I'M GONNA CLEAN UP THE CHRISTIAN SCUM THERE, TOO. I'LL HAVE THEM ALL IN A JERUSALEM PRISON BEFORE YOU CAN BAT AN EYE!

WELL, I'VE TAKEN CARE OF ALL THE HOLIER-THAN-THOU CHRISTIANS HERE—TIME TO BRANCH OUT TO ANOTHER CITY!

SAUL GOT THE LETTER HE WANTED AND SET OFF FOR DAMASCUS. HE HURRIED ALONG THE ROAD WITH A CROWD OF OTHER TRAVELERS. SUDDENLY . . .

WHERE'S THAT LIGHT COMING FROM?

NEVER MIND THE LIGHT—WHERE'S THAT VOICE COMING FROM?

"SAUL, SAUL, WHY ARE YOU PERSECUTING ME?"

WHO SAID THAT?

"I AM JESUS, THE ONE YOU ARE PERSECUTING. NOW GET UP AND GO INTO THE CITY, AND YOU WILL BE TOLD WHAT YOU ARE TO DO."

THE MEN GOT SAUL SETTLED AT JUDAS' HOUSE, THEN WENT ABOUT THEIR BUSINESS.

AFTER SAUL WAS BAPTIZED, HE HAD SOMETHING TO EAT.

SAUL STAYED IN DAMASCUS FOR A FEW MORE DAYS AND BEGAN PREACHING EVERYWHERE HE WENT.

JESUS OF NAZARETH IS THE SON OF GOD!

ISN'T THAT SAUL WHO IS PREACHING ABOUT JESUS?

SAUL? THE GUY WHO ARRESTS ANYONE WHO BELIEVES IN JESUS? YEAH, RIGHT.

LOOK AT THE GUY—IT IS HIM! WHAT HAPPENED TO HIM? HE CAME HERE TO WIPE OUT CHRISTIANS. NOW HE'S ONE OF THEM?

SOON SAUL WAS TRAVELING WITH JESUS' DISCIPLES. EVERYWHERE HE WENT HE PREACHED WITH GREAT POWER AND AUTHORITY ABOUT GOD.

THE NIGHT BEFORE PETER'S TRIAL, HE WAS SLEEPING—CHAINED BETWEEN TWO SOLDIERS. HIS HANDS WERE CHAINED TOGETHER WITH TWO CHAINS. SOLDIERS GUARDED THE DOOR OF HIS CELL.

SUDDENLY, PETER FELT A POKE IN THE SIDE . . .

UHHH, WHAT WAS THAT? WHY IS IT SO BRIGHT IN HERE? IS IT MORNING ALREADY?

AHH—WHO ARE YOU?

QUICK! GET UP!

BUT THE CHAINS ARE . . . OOHH, THE CHAINS JUST FELL OFF MY HANDS!

Taking the Message on the Road

"DEDICATE BARNABAS AND SAUL FOR THE SPECIAL WORK I HAVE FOR THEM."

BARNABAS, SIMEON, LUCIUS, MANAEN AND SAUL WERE WORKING AT THE CHURCH IN ANTIOCH. ONE DAY WHILE THEY WERE WORSHIPING, THE SPIRIT OF GOD SPOKE:

SIMEON, LUCIUS, AND MANAEN FASTED AND PRAYED, THEN LAID HANDS ON BARNABAS AND SAUL, GIVING THEM OVER TO GOD'S SERVICE.

BY THE POWER OF GOD WE RELEASE YOU FROM THE WORK YOU HAVE BEEN DOING FOR THIS CHURCH.

PRAISE GOD!

THE NEXT MORNING THE ROMAN OFFICIALS SENT A MESSENGER TO THE JAIL . . .

IT'S OK TO RELEASE THOSE TWO MEN NOW.

THE JAILER HURRIED TO TELL PAUL AND SILAS.

YOU CAN LEAVE PEACEFULLY NOW. THE ROMANS SAID IT'S OK.

NO WAY! WE'RE ROMAN CITIZENS, AND THEY BEAT US IN PUBLIC WITHOUT A TRIAL.

NOW THEY WANT US TO LEAVE SECRETLY? I DON'T THINK SO. WE WANT A POLICE ESCORT OUT OF THE CITY.

WORD WAS SENT BACK TO THE ROMAN OFFICIALS.

WHAT? THOSE TWO ARE ROMAN CITIZENS?

DIDN'T YOU CHECK THAT OUT BEFORE WE BEAT THEM?

I THOUGHT YOU CHECKED.

YEAH, RIGHT, LIKE IT'S MY JOB.

STOP BICKERING. LET'S JUST GET THEM OUT OF TOWN AS QUICKLY AS WE CAN.

THE ROMAN OFFICIALS APOLOGIZED TO PAUL AND SILAS AND PUBLICLY ESCORTED THEM OUT OF TOWN.

TEACH, PAUL, WE WANT TO HEAR WHAT YOU HAVE TO SAY. WE'LL LISTEN AS LONG AS YOU WANT TO TALK.

THE CROWD OF PEOPLE SETTLED DOWN IN A ROOM ON THE THIRD FLOOR OF A HOUSE. IT WAS DIMLY LIT, THOUGH SEVERAL LAMPS WERE BURNING. THE ROOM WAS WARM AND A LITTLE SMOKY BECAUSE OF THE LAMPS.
ONE YOUNG MAN SAT DOWN ON THE LEDGE OF AN OPEN WINDOW.

THIS IS A GOOD SPOT. I CAN HEAR PAUL AND GET A LITTLE FRESH AIR AT THE SAME TIME.

HE'S DEAD!

PAUL WAS RIGHT BEHIND THEM. HE KNELT DOWN AND GENTLY PICKED UP THE YOUNG MAN.

DON'T WORRY, THIS BOY IS ALIVE.

SUDDENLY EUTYCHUS OPENED HIS EYES. HE WAS ALIVE AGAIN! HE WENT BACK UPSTAIRS AND ATE AND LISTENED TO PAUL PREACH UNTIL SUNRISE.

COME ON, BOY, PAUL'S FINISHED. I'LL TAKE YOU HOME.

GLAD YOU'RE OK, EUTYCHUS.

YEAH, CLOSE CALL.

MORE THAN FORTY MEN JOINED TOGETHER TO MAKE THIS VOW. THEN THEY WENT TO THE CHIEF PRIESTS AND LEADERS OF THE PEOPLE.

WE'VE PROMISED EACH OTHER AND GOD THAT WE WON'T EAT OR DRINK ANYTHING UNTIL PAUL IS DEAD. BUT WE NEED YOUR HELP. HERE'S OUR PLAN . . .

WE WANT YOU TO GO TO THE ROMAN OFFICER AND SAY YOU NEED MORE INFORMATION ABOUT PAUL. MAKE IT LOOK CONVINCING, LIKE YOU REALLY DO NEED TO KNOW MORE ABOUT HIM.

WHEN THEY BRING HIM OUT OF PRISON, WE'LL BE WAITING. BELIEVE ME, WE'LL MAKE SURE HE NEVER GETS TO YOU!

WHAT THE MEN DIDN'T KNOW WAS THAT PAUL'S NEPHEW HEARD THEIR ENTIRE PLAN. HE HURRIED TO WARN PAUL.

IT'S A TRICK, UNCLE PAUL. THEY'RE GONNA KILL YOU!

PAUL KNEW EXACTLY WHAT TO DO.

Shipwreck!

ACTS 27:1–28:31

GOVERNOR FELIX HEARD THE ACCUSATIONS AGAINST PAUL AND FELT THEY WERE TOO WEAK TO CONVICT HIM. FELIX WOULD HAVE SET PAUL FREE EXCEPT THAT PAUL HAD REQUESTED TO HAVE HIS CASE HEARD BY THE EMPEROR IN ROME.

SO, ALONG WITH MANY OTHER PRISONERS, PAUL WAS PUT ON A PRISON SHIP WHICH WAS SAILING TO ITALY.

A LITTLE WAY INTO THE JOURNEY, PROBLEMS DEVELOPED . . .

The Best is Yet to Be

REVELATION 21–22

When Jesus went back to heaven he promised his followers that someday he would come back for them. Everyone who believes in Jesus will go to heaven to live with Jesus forever.

God talked to one of Jesus' followers, John, in a dream. He showed John what heaven will be like.

Heaven will be as beautiful as a bride dressed in her beautiful white wedding gown. It will be filled with all people who love God.

Heaven will be a happy place. There won't be any sadness there, no crying, no sickness or pain. We won't have to worry about crimes because there won't be any sin in heaven. God won't allow people into heaven who are murderers or do bad things; and there will definitely be no people who worship idols. All those people will spend forever in a lake of burning fire.

There will be a new city in heaven filled with jewels. It will have streets paved with pure gold.

The new city will always be filled with light. There will be no darkness because the glory of God will light everything.

The best part of heaven will be that God is there all the time. We can talk to him anytime we want to.

John wrote down everything God told him about heaven. It's all in the last book of the Bible, which is called Revelation. He wanted believers to know about the future—the hope of spending forever in heaven with God.

John wrote that . . . Jesus said, I am coming soon and my reward is with me to repay all according to their deeds.

All the people who love Jesus—who have ever loved Jesus—will be with him in heaven one day.

John's last words, in fact some of the last words in the Bible are Come, Lord Jesus! The grace of the Lord Jesus be with you all.